Hope for the Situationally Disorganized

by DL Ashley

Confusion Solution®

Illustrations by Amber Leigh Luecke

Published by Confusion Solution
First Edition: August 3, 2021

ISBN:978-1-0879-3728-1 (Hardback)

Dedication

This book is dedicated to my sister Debbie and her husband Scott

who encouraged me to give birth to Confusion Solution.

To my extremely experienced business partner,

Ninna Atkins, Decluttered and Beyond, from whom I have learned and grown.

Table of Contents

The Situation is This...

You wake up at five o'clock in the morning, put on coffee, maybe have a cup yourself, start breakfast, try to wake any others in the house, try to motivate everyone to get dressed and moving, try to get them to eat breakfast, fix their lunches, and shuffle them out the door, or take them wherever they need to be. You then start getting yourself and your partner (if you have one) ready to go to work outside the home, get showered, dressed, grab a protein bar, papers, purses, keys, sunglasses, sweaters, and anything else you might need while away, then get in the car(s), and go off to work, unless you work from home which has its own unique list of responsibilities.

Whew!

But wait, it's not over...

You do your job, get in your car to come home at the end of the day (unless you work from home), maybe pick up something for dinner, or pick up a kid (if you have one), go home, fix dinner for the family, take a kid to an event, stay for the event, go home, make kids do homework, maybe you have homework, try to motivate everyone to do their homework, argue about staying up late, argue about whether kids can use their computers for the next three hours, finally get everyone to bed, clean up the kitchen, look at your partner and sigh.

We all lead busy lives trying to fit too much into each day. Wouldn't it be nice if our busy schedules were a little more flexible? Wouldn't it be nice if we had more time? What if something unexpected comes up? Are we prepared?

Our routines are already hectic. So, when something extraordinary happens to change the way we operate, we are blindsided and our typically ordered day is now off-balance leaving us with even less time, a full load, and we don't always know how to adapt.

We become scattered, our things become scattered, and our time is subject to loss which can ultimately result in being situationally disorganized leaving us feeling like things are spinning out-of-control. There is little to guide us as to what to do first and we need order to prevent us from shutting down and becoming exhausted when surprises interrupt our day.

Most interruptions don't require radical adjustments because they could simply be that Susie's dance class was postponed or unexpected guests have come to visit. Small changes don't give us pause because we can cope and easily rearrange our schedules. We also know that in just a short while we will be back into the safety of our normal way of being. However, adjusting to more serious changes like an unexpected illness or emergency travel for work can lead to frustration. These types of disruptions bring normal to a halt. We have to adjust how we handle our responsibilities and that means our schedules have to change. It starts with our current situation and ends in the celebration of our achievements.

For all of us who struggle with being Out-of-Order, we can avoid agonizing about the obstacles we face that prevent us from coping. This book was written to provide hope and will examine our routines, how to plan to avoid confusion, and how to focus on what to do when changes arise. It will open up ideas for learning who we are, how we manage our time, and how to adjust so we can enjoy a more organized lifestyle.

For all of us who struggle with being Out-of-Order, we can avoid agonizing about the obstacles we face that prevent us from coping.

Avoiding the Situationally Disorganized Condition

How do we avoid the condition? Well, it means reorganizing our routine and shifting our responsibilities to allow time in each day to effectively handle interruptions. It means prioritizing, restructuring, and reviewing how we manage our time to reduce the stress of trying to beat the clock or tackling unrealistic projects. It means learning to recognize the impact change has on our ability to accomplish our responsibilities.

None of us want our lives to be out-of-order. We don't want the mess or the disorientation but, we are usually way too busy to contemplate alternatives that will help us muddle through. When we look at improving our routine we begin to see things in a new perspective and that is when we can effectively get our lives back to normal.

It is important to note that having an organized routine brings with it many opportunities that encourage us and keep us encouraged. It is these benefits that help us...

- Become less burdened.

- Embrace change.

- Have clarity.

- Expose free time.

- Save money.

- Improve efficiency.

We get frustrated when things aren't going according to plan. We don't want to be situationally disorganized. So the best method for establishing and maintaining order when we are faced with change is to be organized in the first place.

I know, I know. This probably sounds easier than it is doable but if we take a serious look at what we have to do and how we do things, we are better prepared to handle change without the undue stress of waiting until we can resume what has been normal in the past.

We have to find new methods of approaching change. Feeling out-of-order isn't permanent but when faced with disruptions to our day, we experience an immediate impact that can become overwhelming. We may even find that the biggest change we have to make is our willingness to change our behavior.

If we think change is bad, then it will be. If we think change brings opportunities, then it will.

What? Me, Change?

I know this isn't what you want to hear but it just may be what you need to consider to be able to effectively deal with getting your life back on track. Our goals for order demand change and that requires us to be open so we can determine better ways to address how to make those changes. And realize, too, there is work to be done to regain control. It means taking time to ask ourselves what causes us to behave the way we do when handling change because our behavior can hinder us from taking action.

It doesn't mean we have to change who we are, it just means that realizing we can do things a bit differently gives us options that will help to improve the time spent on getting things done. Getting unstuck is up to us. There will be decisions we have to make to avoid becoming situationally disorganized. Changing how we respond to change is powerful and when we decide to make the effort toward improvement and embrace change, we are unstoppable.

However, altering our behavior isn't always easy, it takes discipline. We now not only have to make decisions about how to change our routine but identify how we function daily and in a crisis. We have to take a step back and think with an open mind about the way we do things because, on the upside, it isn't unusual to develop new habits naturally. The circumstances that we are faced with when change occurs help us to change. For instance, you may typically be used to starting your day at a certain time but now have been tasked with taking Susie to school because her schedule has changed and she can no longer take the bus. What do you do? You start your day earlier, of course. What is the result? You change your behavior based on the circumstances.

We have to be open so that when we encounter change it doesn't stop us. We want change to create a desire for new ways to operate during our day. We want to become more flexible and better able to organize our thoughts. Re-evaluating how we approach change keeps us from stumbling and allows our habits to evolve.

Changing doesn't have to be difficult. It's important to not let fear or frustration get to us because most interruptions are only temporary even if we may not see an immediate end. Our inability to manage everything may make us feel lost but knowing that our situation isn't permanent will help us put our time into perspective.

If we think change is bad, then it will be. If we think change brings opportunities, then it will. It's all up to us to do what we can to avoid becoming situationally disorganized and be more productive. Once we recognize that the habits we allow to deter us from our goal need changing, it is then that we begin to find solutions.

By becoming aware of how and why we do what we do, that is when we can change our patterns of behavior and begin to see that time slows and life becomes less hectic. Knowing that change occurs and accepting that fact will lessen the stress, because change will happen. That's one thing you can depend on.

Creating a New Strategy

In order to get in order, creating a plan or a to-do list for what we want to accomplish keeps us focused and is essential to managing time. It helps remind us of our commitments and by revising our routine we inevitably change our future way of doing things.

You will want to write everything down. So, before you begin, invest in a journal, planner, or calendar for capturing and organizing your goals. Just make sure whatever you use has enough room for dates, notes, and allows for the ability to make changes. This is also a great opportunity to explore your stationery store or research online for supplies to help motivate you and make the process more enjoyable.

The first thing necessary to create an effective plan is to carve out uninterrupted time away from family, work, and cell phones. We need to concentrate on making practical decisions regarding how we spend our time. We want to be realistic and detailed about what we ultimately want to achieve and estimate the time required to complete each goal. This applies not only to what we do on a daily basis but on future goals, as well.

Once goals are defined and written down, then put them in order of importance. Taking kids to school might be more important than going for a run. It all depends on timing and necessity but only you can determine which item on your list is a priority. Just the process of writing down our goals increases our awareness of what's important. It is the process of discovery that helps us consider devoting more time to taking care of our responsibilities, family and friends, and ourselves. Prioritizing responsibilities gives us the tools we need to make the right adjustments to our schedule in the event of change.

Re-examine your current routine to see where you can lessen the time you spend on each of your responsibilities. Give this part of your plan serious thought. Try to think about alternating days where possible or assigning responsibilities, that rob you of time, to others to handle. Trying to do everything at the same time or alone will only set you down the path to being out-of-order. Considering the things you currently do is a good basis for creating a new structure. You will notice where you spend the most time and how to juggle responsibilities to give you more time. When you break free of normal and risk change, you create a new vision for maneuvering through your day. The risk you think you are taking is small in comparison to the impact it will have on your obligations, social interactions, and your time.

The next step is to look into the details that are necessary to complete your goals. This may not seem important since taking out the trash is pretty logical and doesn't require too much detail. The point here is to identify what goes into each task beyond the obvious. For instance, if one of your goals is to remodel your kitchen then you would write down specifically all that goes into making that happen. Add approximately how long each task might take and what materials you will need or which contractors to hire. The more you are aware of what is involved to meet your goals the more realistic your routine will be and you are better prepared to follow through.

Reconstructing your routine is also the beginning of influencing your behavior. The more you give yourself permission to change, the more you will recognize the power you have to control your environment. The benefit of re-evaluating your commitments is that you will have direction and the process leads to entertaining new ideas and experiencing new ways of living.

Your plan should consist of daily responsibilities that are necessary to maintaining order like, washing dishes, walking the dog, or going to the grocery store, but keep in mind that not everything in your plan has to be a chore. It should include things you want to do. You need to include time for things that build you up. Pleasant diversions are necessary to ease the pressures that can come from an overly structured lifestyle. Spending time on the phone with family and friends, or taking a much-needed shopping day or walk can be the type of thing that allows you to survive during turmoil. When faced with interruptions to your routine remember to update your to-do list each time you accomplish a goal.

Our time is invaluable. We try to capture its fleeting moments with the utmost effort in an attempt to create more of it, or at least make it have meaning. It is our lack of understanding about the advantages of planning that can prohibit us from fully enjoying our day. We take on what we need to at the moment of demand and rarely consider the process of developing a more productive direction leaving us in a situation that feels out-of-control.

An example of a structured plan may look something like this:

Your main objective indicates what you ultimately want to accomplish.

Main Objective
I want to be able to park my car in the garage.

Main Objective
I want to be able to park my car in the garage.

My Commitment
Start Date: August 1
Completion Date: August 15

Add commitment dates for starting and completing your project.

TASKS

Tasks are details for what you need to complete your goals.

1. Assess what's in the garage.

2. Remove items from shelves and pull items from floor locations and sort by category.

3. Elim...

TASKS	TIME	HELP
1. Assess what's in the garage.	15 min	
...pull items ...ory.	2 hrs	Steve
...ve items	...hrs	Steve

Include realistic times and the names of people who might assist you.

MATERIALS

1. Containers, bags and/or boxes
2. Markers
3. Measuring tape
4. Pegboard and pegs
5. Hooks
6. Bungee cords
7. Shelving

Materials may be required, so list what you think you will need so you are prepared.

Planning does require a bit of brain work. You have to think about all the steps you need to follow to get to where you are capable of managing your responsibilities efficiently in the event of change. Discovering how you want to achieve your goals will be evident and more easily attainable as you write them down.

20

Where Do I Go From Here?

We have looked at how to organize our time so now let's turn our attention to organizing our things.

We have included maintaining our home as an essential part of our plan so it will be easier to stay organized when our routine is interrupted. The way we function is the product of our current situation. What is it that is causing us to feel organizationally challenged?

Are we:

- Cluttered and unsure how to organize excess items that have no home or continue to find themselves out of place?

- Overwhelmed and have too much and are experiencing anxiety and frustration?

- Time deficient and have difficulty managing schedules to include personal time and organizing projects?

- Emotionally attached and have difficulty sorting through items that have been collected through travel or personal history?

- Financially attached and have difficulty sorting through items that you have invested in financially?

- Document challenged and are lacking awareness of how to manage paperwork?

- Unmotivated and simply refuse or lack the energy to accomplish goals?

- Difficulty seeking help because unsure of the role outside support should play?

These are ways of thinking that restrict us from focusing on possible opportunities to fully experience the potential of an organized lifestyle. There are many reasons why it is difficult for us to change. We become out-of-order because...

- Living in an environment that causes an individual to feel as if things are out-of-control can result in loss of motivation, difficulty making decisions, time evaporation, dysfunction, and possibly physical or psychological harm.

- We are the product of a society that has suffered, in the past, deep financial despair and the boom of an industrial revolution. These are events that instilled a desire for us to never again realize the pain of doing without.

- We have acquired, accumulated, substituted, purchased, and saved without considering the space we need to house it or even, in some cases, reasons for acquiring, accumulating, substituting, purchasing, and saving.

- Eventually, we will have to deal with the overages we have accumulated which will require taking a deeper look into the value of the things we treasure and what to do with them.

- We don't adjust well to change.

- We don't know how to look for opportunities that will give us that coveted spark of motivation and knowledge.

- We just don't have enough time.

Don't Worry, be hopeful.

Logic and Order

Creating order is a logical process. Whether we are organizing our thoughts, or our things, logic plays a significant role. And, as with logic, organizing is the process of using a systematic series of steps to arrive at a conclusion. It is the arrangement of things according to special sequences, patterns, or use. The ability to use logic, in organizing, creates perfect placement for our belongings to add benefit to the way we live and work. Both processes complement each other because, without logic there can be no order and without order we miss out on the advantages of logical solutions.

We are attached to what we own and making logical decisions about changing our perspective on placement and order is sometimes difficult. Precise attention to what we consider most important and how it's used produces a more effective outcome. It is our own individual assessment that will make sense of usage and arrangement. Whether it's organizing our desk or sorting our junk drawer, putting things in order is uniquely the logic of the owner. It has to make sense to the user. There is no one way to put things in order just as there is no one way for the logical mind to consider being disorganized. Since the logical process of arrangement depends on the owner, it does not depend on the expectations of others.

A perfect example of this came about from a project I worked on with a client. I was challenged with putting books and papers in order which were definitely in need of organization according to my well-trained eye. But I soon learned that my eyes needed adjusting. What I assumed was a logical approach to putting things in order wasn't the way my client felt would be efficient. I needed to listen and understand what was important to him. I needed to adapt my organizing style to complement his method of working. My experience didn't matter, at that point, because it was how he needed his space to be that would be logical to him.

Allowing him to explain his expectations was key to developing a system that would create productivity. It would have to be a system that was not the result of placing things in order by categories, as I saw them, but order according to his perception of order, his logic. It was about how he reasoned and made sense of the materials he needed within his reach. It was order by each topic he needed to access at any one given point in the evolution of his research.

It wasn't pretty. It didn't maximize space, and it was continually changing. But, the concept was logical to this incredibly intelligent individual and it would have been far more frustrating for both of us if I tried to fit him into a clichéd or predetermined sense of order.

Creating a balance between emotion and logic is important when it comes to making decisions.

Emotions can also influence our approach to coming up with logical solutions. What we are emotionally invested in doesn't always mean we will look for practical, effective placement, or release for increasing space, but places the emphasis on appearance and display because of our sentimental attachment. Sometimes our feelings will result in our inability to focus on our primary goal for order and can result in the absence of logic. However, emotion and logic can work hand-in-hand and both should influence our decisions, just not to the point of one over-riding the other. For instance, if logic dictates what we consider is the proper location or arrangement of something, we may become inflexible and lack the ability to change. While being too emotional, we may end up not making changes at all. This doesn't mean that organizing our sentimental accumulations is done without using logic. It just means that we have a tendency to avoid a systematic logical approach to putting things in order because of our emotional attachment.

The organizing process requires communication and possibly compromise. Creating a balance between emotion and logic is important when it comes to making decisions. And even more so when there are other people to consider.

We have learned from our jobs that logic has a powerful impact on our ability to handle problems. The demands of business instill a get-to-the-point attitude using logical organizational skills for making critical decisions in order to reduce risk. This structure is based on the principle that to effectively explain or present a point-of-view, it is important to be concise and time-sensitive. It focuses on weeding out information that isn't pertinent to reaching the end goal. By paring down our speak to convey only the most significant reasons for our ideas we encourage concentration from our audience.

One example of how we can use this process in our day-to-day lives is when we are trying to organize our calendar. The emphasis would be focused on the most basic commitments eliminating the details surrounding each event, unlike our plan development where the details are necessary to set goals and priorities. It isn't logical to spend time on details when the overall goal of our calendar can be met efficiently using simple reminders.

The point of using logic is to minimize our approach to how things are organized and keep them organized. If we attempt to reach our goals for order by focusing on their use and accessibility we will discover effective, manageable placement.

Motivation

After you have committed to your plan, getting the motivation to implement your plan is just as important. Motivation is the enthusiasm that boosts our ability to dig in. If we are not motivated the time we have estimated to complete our goals will become unrealistic. Face it, getting started requires effort. If you think your routine is an opportunity for a more manageable lifestyle, that can be motivating in itself.

We often need other influences or materials that make the process easy to not only get us enthused but to guide us to a rewarding end. We are always motivated when we are getting ready to do something we enjoy. If we aren't into the task we will do everything we can to avoid it. A few simple ideas for making our job more enjoyable may be all the help we need. Here are a few suggestions to inspire creativity.

- Schedule some uninterrupted time, now and then, to sit down and review your goals. Just reminding yourself of what you want to accomplish will be encouraging.

- Music is a positive choice to get you up and moving. Put on something with a beat and turn it up. Even if you are not initially affected, just waiting a few minutes will stimulate and give you the energy you need to move.

- Shopping can be a motivator as long as you are buying something necessary to complete a task. Be sure you have the time to add shopping to your routine because a few new essentials can help motivate you. And, well, it's shopping, after all.

- Incentivize yourself by creating clever games to take care of smaller tasks. One idea is to spend a few minutes in one room gathering items that belong in another room and put them in the room where they belong. Don't put them away, just yet. Then pick up something from that room and repeat the process. You have now just accomplished a small task that will make it easier to concentrate on the more detailed assignment of placing the items you gathered in their proper places.

- If you are having a hard time getting started on your organizing project, use the 15-minute rule. This means you will only work on your project 15 minutes at a time. You can allow more time but not less. When your 15 minutes is up do something else for 15 minutes. Then go back to your organizing project and repeat the process until your project is complete. You will be amazed to see how much can be accomplished in these short sessions, and most often you will find yourself continuing to work longer than 15 minutes because increased motivation kicks in as you continue.

- Involving family members is a great way to encourage motivation. Plan an event. Assign each person a task. Make invitations with the date and time for your organizing event. Write out instructions for their areas of responsibility and give them containers, bags, markers, and a timeline to complete their project. Then, when each project is completed, reward them with a movie or a walk. Get away from the house for a while to clear your mind and refocus. Just remember to clean up before you leave so you don't have to face an unfinished job when you return.

- Motivate your kids to help organize by putting buttons or stickers in hidden places. Let them know what project they will be working on each time they find a button or sticker. Then send them on their hunt.

- Set up a reward system for yourself. Think about buying a new piece of art or allowing yourself some personal time. Giving yourself a reward for your achievements motivates you to follow-through.

- Motivate yourself by calling in a housekeeper to clean your home. This will free you from having to deal with the normal day-to-day chores that distract you and keep you from getting more important things taken care of.

Permit yourself to stop if a task becomes too burdensome. You want to stay motivated and that means allowing time to take a break. Unless your projects are time-sensitive, like keeping a scheduled appointment, there is no requirement for you to finish what you have started if it isn't a priority. Be as flexible now as you were in the planning stages. Your responsibilities will be met with a more positive attitude.

It takes time to embrace change so allow yourself to go back, look at your progress and ask yourself if you are keeping on track, and consider making necessary adjustments. It's a waste of your time if you fall back into old habits so remind yourself of all you have accomplished.

It's a waste of your time if you fall back into old habits so remind yourself of all you have accomplished.

Knowing Why and What To Do About It

The key to effective organizing is knowing. Whether you are trying to declutter or downsize, you have to know what you own, know how to use what you own, and know where to find what you own. It also helps to know why we do things a certain way and what we can do to change it.

Space

Space is an opportunity, and in some cases, a luxury. It can confuse us when we realize we don't know how to gain more space or utilize it better. Our shelves and walls have so much on them that they draw attention away from conversations, or study, or creativity. We can lose focus when we are surrounded by so much stuff. That is when we inevitably look for ways to accommodate what we own. We buy shelving systems, furniture, and storage containers but adding more isn't dealing with overcrowding. Unfortunately, when we design our homes or purchase our furnishings we don't consider if they will adequately accommodate our belongings or that we have allowed for expansion that is required as we continue to accumulate.

We can't stand to have a blank wall, an empty shelf or drawer and we all suffer from this. Sometimes it's wanting to display what we have purchased or created for our friends and families to view. Sometimes it's that we feel we are supposed to take advantage of blank space and look to fill it with something, anything. In the case of work, we love to put things on walls and desktops as a reminder of where we want to be, who we love, and our accomplishments. But when there is limited space in an office environment it can quickly become cluttered and unproductive.

We all collect. That can mean anything from teaspoons to clothing and there is nothing wrong with having things out and on display until we run out of space. And, it still isn't wrong until overcrowding and lack of space creates a hazardous environment for us or others.

When space is at a premium, there is a huge variety of items that you can buy to accommodate the need for extra storage. Just make sure to plan what to buy based on not only what is in the space now, but what you will probably purchase in the future and remember pretty isn't always functional. Each cabinet or shelf system needs to effectively accommodate your things and you need to be sure the furnishings will fit your living space efficiently before you buy.

Also, look into revamping storage you currently have. Maybe that chest of drawers could be used elsewhere and for something other than clothes. It also doesn't have to be expensive to be effective and look nice.

Just as with buying furniture, storage containers need our assessment of what we want to be stored before we buy. We can go a little bit container happy when we see how inexpensive containers are because there is such a large selection out there to choose from. There are drawer dividers, kitchen organizers, garage totes, shoe boxes, file boxes, closet organizers, food containers, and the list goes on. It's wonderful to know that we have so many options for creating and managing our space. Just spend wisely.

If we have room, we buy, if we don't have room, we still buy. We can change that behavior if we consider what we need and where we are going to store it before we buy. It's not an easy change, but we can do small things that will lead us in that direction.

There is always space, we just can't always see it. Simple adjustments to books on a shelf, or clothes hanging in a closet reveal space we never thought we had. It's okay to occupy space with our collections but using common sense and minimizing placement or finding proper storage are options that will improve the use of the space you already have. True minimalism doesn't always come naturally. It needs a gentle push

Sorting

To handle over-accumulation, it is necessary to sort through what you have so you can make calculated decisions about what you want to keep, donate, or sell.

Decision-making is probably the most difficult part of any organizing project so, make sorting your belongings easier by gathering some basic materials to use in the process...

- Markers

- Large bags for trash or donations

- Boxes or containers for things you want to keep or sell

- A box or container for things when you can't make an immediate decision

The purpose of effective sorting is to allow for quick decisions that make the best use of your time. If you can't decide what to do with an item right away an 'I-Don't-Know' box or container will give you a place to keep things until you have more time to focus on whether to keep or release. There will come a time when a decision needs to be made, but maybe just not right now.

Sorting before you put things away will save you countless organizing hours because you will have identified what you own and evaluated the space where they will reside in the end. Being prepared will get the job done more efficiently.

Contact homeless shelters or thrift stores to find out what they will and won't take. Call local utility companies to find out what you're allowed to recycle and where, if you can put items in the trash for pick up, and what's the best way to get rid of hazardous waste.

Create a resource list of places to take donations or recycle so you don't have to stop during the sorting process. Tag or label each bag or box, as they are filled, with their destination. This will make distributing your items easier at the end of your project.

If making decisions about what things to keep or to give away is too difficult then I recommend you keep them, at least temporarily. There is no right or wrong time to release your hold on something you have purchased or have been given. It doesn't matter if you have kept it for six months or a year. And there is no reason to experience loss if it isn't necessary.

Before you decide what to release, consider the impact of continuing to keep and avoid second guesses.

Ask yourself:

- Is it necessary?

- Does it still provide solutions for what it was originally intended to provide?

- Is it broken or torn and no longer usable?

- Is it safe to continue to use?

- Does it represent a memorable time in your life?

- Do you have more than one?

Releasing

The value we place on what we own is measured by the dollars we have spent, our memories, and the gifts we have been given. It isn't easy to part with those things we have invested in, or have cherished from our adventures, or received from the kindness of others. As with changes that affect our routines, so do situations and time affect the value of what we own. Our priorities shift giving us the opportunity for a fresh perspective.

If you are thinking you can sell what you own, consider the time you invest in trying to set up a sale is often worth much more than the profit you anticipate you will gain. If you still want to sell what you no longer need then make it an event. Invite others who have things to sell. At least your focus won't be on how much money you will make but simply on having a good time. In any event, do not bring the items back inside if they do not sell. Find other ways to distribute them instead of continuing to hang on. Consider this could be an opportunity to make a donation to a local charity and let it serve a purpose in someone else's life.

It's okay to let go of anything that no longer has meaning.

As we live we might decide to have children, go on vacations, enjoy special holidays, or just have life experiences that we want to remember. Keeping things that remind us of good times isn't a bad thing. Our memories are things that we can share with family and friends or pass down to other generations to remind them of our history. It's just a good idea to organize them and store them away from areas that are more useful for other things.

As for the gifts we are given by those we love, there comes a time when certain items become more of a burden to hang on to. For instance, a gift that someone gave you but there is no memory of who gave it to you is far different from gifts that were given to you by your grand-parents or significant other. It's okay to let go of anything that no longer has meaning. No one will think less of you if you give away that crystal bowl that was given to you by who knows who at your wedding 25 years ago. Take a picture, and, you've heard it before, it will last longer.

Help From the Outside

When we start a home organizing project, we must be aware that being organized means different things to different people. There is no one way to keep and store what we own. We search for ideas and direction from others but can get trapped into thinking someone else's idea of organizing is right for us. Family and friends mean well but sometimes their willingness to help can get in the way when deciding what to keep. When we are told how to do things by those we care about we often rebel causing hurt feelings. So, allow yourself to listen and be open even if you don't agree. Keep in mind that being organized is knowing what you have and where you keep things and you are the only one who can determine what that should look like.

Other outside sources can be influential in providing guidelines and the basis for considering how we will reach a logical conclusion. However, it is our own unique lifestyle that has the most impact on our logical approach to order. We all may have similar ideas regarding where things should be placed but how we actually organize them depends on our point-of-view. For instance, we may agree that there are logical places for our things like pantries for our canned goods or drawers for our utensils, but how those things are organized within those places is solely up to us. It is logical to put all our tools together in one place, maybe a garage, a workshop, or a toolbox, but the order in which tools are placed in those locations may seem logical to one person and not another. How we use an item and how often we use it will indicate its placement and accessibility.

*Seeking help isn't a sign
of vulnerability,
it is a sign of self-respect.*

Being Tidy

We have probably been told that organizing means our homes should be neat and tidy. But, being tidy doesn't necessarily mean we are organized. Being organized simply means putting our things in order. We can always close a closet door or shut the lid on a container that houses a variety of things but open that door or remove that lid and it will probably be evident that what has been hidden there is not in order at all. Neat, clean, and tidy contribute to maintaining order but they are not always as in-tune with the organizing process.

Documents

Managing paperwork is another point where we stop trying to get organized. The documents we keep are often not necessary to hold on to. Things that show we have something of value like, our home, our vehicles, our medical records, or our investments should be kept until they no longer apply. For instance, if we sell a car, the legal holding on that car is no longer our responsibility. The best way to find out what is important to keep is to consult with a certified public accountant. The IRS has recommendations, as well, by searching 'How long do I keep my documents?', on their site www.irs.gov.

Clichés

Finally, don't let clichés make your decisions for you. It doesn't matter how long you have had something and never wear it. If you keep your wedding dress or your high school sweater it's probably been there a while and just because you don't wear it doesn't mean you have to toss it out. Time should not be the determining factor in letting something go. That piece of clothing may be timeless or a classic but once you have stumbled upon it this is your opportunity to decide whether you will wear it or not. Being old or vintage doesn't mean you can't keep it. It simply means that it's old or vintage. There are many ways for how to manage items we no longer need, just because it's old or you haven't seen it in a while doesn't mean it doesn't hold personal value. Recognize its worth alone not how old it is.

You don't need to get rid of something you haven't used in a specific time. This suggests you actually went out and thoughtlessly spent your money on something you needed or thought you might need. I mean, it's wise to buy a plunger, but that doesn't mean you have to use it or that you have used it. It means that it is a good idea to have one around. Yes, maybe having three or four is unnecessary, but how long you have had your things shouldn't be the sole factor for getting rid of them. Scheduling time to review will lead to decisions that you can feel confident in making. So, I suggest, if you haven't worn it or used it in a certain length of time re-evaluate it.

Just be careful that you are not a slave to clichés that can interfere with logic.

The statement *"out-of-sight, out-of-mind"* suggests that if it isn't on display then we have freed ourselves of having to deal with it. We are essentially trying to hide things from view that we don't want to consider may need to be addressed, but then we forget we have them over time. However, some things we own are just best put out of sight. You know where you keep your underwear so no one will see it, you know where to keep your legal documents, you know where your kitchen utensils are stored. The point here is knowing. When you store or organize things in containers or drawers you will know where they are. It doesn't mean you won't deal with them once they are put away. They, of course, need to be hidden in an orderly fashion and not just thrown into a closed space. Knowing what is out-of-sight isn't necessarily out-of-mind.

"It-is-what-it-is" is a statement used often to relieve us when we feel trapped. It finalizes difficult circumstances that we feel are unchangeable. That is a true statement if you have no option to influence change. However, we say it often and without thought when there is an opportunity for change. We just tend to stop looking for options by simply stating that *"it-is-what-it-is"* and that's all we can do.

Just be careful that you are not a slave to clichés that can interfere with logic. While they may be true in some cases, they don't apply to everything or everyone.

Organizing Stressors

Feeling out-of-order is stressful. Trying to be more organized is also stressful. It comes from not knowing what to do, what we will find, or how to decide. It is exasperating when our kitchen counter or other furnishings are covered with stuff and we don't have the energy or the know-how to clear away the clutter.

The list of things that need to be done in preparation for large changes can feel unsurmountable. We already have too much to do without the addition of major changes to our routine. But, be encouraged because preparing for a move, planning a wedding, or adding a person to our lives, whether it's a baby or a partner, are opportunities for new perspectives.

If we are moving, there are materials we need to buy to help us pack in an organized and safe fashion. There are things to have turned on and things to have turned off, things that require us to schedule transportation, and a plan to put it all into action. Then there are all the things we have to do once we are in our new place.

Enlarging our family or planning seasonal gatherings can be stressful. We have to become aware of how much space we will need to accommodate an event or an addition to our brood. It also means our routine must include a change to our financial obligations. Consider the time involved with this type of change and understand that other responsibilities will have to be placed on hold or assigned to other people, and in some cases that may require permanent changes to our routine.

Preparing for college or changing careers are other areas of our lives that require a great deal of planning. It's not simply attending a new school or starting our day in a new place. It's searching for the right institution or job opportunity, travel, submitting documents, and so much more. These are interruptions that can impact an entire family. Even though the process is temporary the work is for a long-term dynamic result.

Experiencing the loss of a loved one will stop your world. Sadness consumes us long after the funeral is over and sorting through a closet or a storage space only represents pain, duty, and resentment which can cause anxiety.

This would be the last time she would set aside a day to go through her husband's things, or at least that's what she told herself. As she sat on the end of her bed, hands clenched at her sides, facing her husband's closet door, the voices of well meaning friends and family resounded in her head telling her it was time. An empty cardboard box lay on the floor next to her open and waiting to be filled with the very personal things she felt belonged in that closet forever. She drew a deep breath and stood. She reached out a hand and turned the knob. As the door swung open she was hit with emotions and memories that brought tears to her eyes. She backed up, closed the door, turned and kicked the box across the bedroom floor.

There is no time limit that can be placed on when to begin the physical detachment process just as there is no time limit that can be placed on how long we need to grieve.

We need to wait and rest in our loss. By waiting, we can avoid making rash decisions about what to do with things that we are emotionally attached to, and know that when the time is right, it will be liberating. We will never truly let go of our grief. We can only try and live around it knowing, too, that we have only let go of things and not the respect and admiration of someone no longer with us

There are so many elements to organizing that can lead to exhaustion but there are ways to conquer the problem. Even the most stressful of situations can be relieved with time, focus, and planning. While introducing a new family member into the mix is not necessarily a temporary situation, events are. Being careful to recognize the difference puts us at ease. We worry about so much in our daily lives, where to go, what to do, and how to survive. The fact that once we have decided to change, we prepare ourselves for the unexpected and lessen stress.

Alternatives for the Situationally Disorganized

We all want to make our tasks as easy to accomplish as possible especially when our time is limited. We just have to think of alternatives and get creative.

Ask yourself what you are doing that takes up your time. In normal situations folding your clothes is an excellent way to stay organized but do you really need to fold everything? If you want or feel like you are supposed to fold your clothes but don't have time...then don't. That's right, I said it.

Think about what items actually need to be folded. I mean, really, socks? Buy a container or decorative basket for each person and when the socks come out of the dryer put them right into the basket. Everyone in your family probably knows how to match socks so give them some credit for not grabbing the blue one to go with the argyle one. However, there may be exceptions, so giving a little direction is okay.

Hang clothes whenever possible. Hanging is a more efficient use of your time versus folding. If you don't have a lot of hanging space look for ways to double up. Combine outfits or layer pants on a hanger. Bulky items like sweaters, towels, and blankets should be folded but if that's all you need to fold then good for you.

As for the mail? Why, put it on the dining room table or kitchen counter, of course. Just kidding. You can reduce the urge by setting a basket by the front door to drop off incoming mail. You will have to set aside a specific time regularly to go through it and pull out important documents like bills, but, in the meantime, your mail isn't scattered about creating clutter. Baskets are awesome for other things, as well. They can accommodate shoes, toys, magazines, and anything else that tends to lie around when in a rush. Simply providing alternative ways of looking at your disorder will help you maintain order.

Get help! While you are used to taking care of things yourself there are others out there that can help carry the load. Ask for help with transportation issues, or running errands, or hire the neighbor kid to mow your lawn. Many people are willing to help when your routine is no longer manageable. Just set your pride aside and let them.

Take advantage of outside services that can help in time of need like:

- putting mail on hold.

- using public transportation.

- hiring housekeepers, event planners, and caregivers.

- temporarily subscribe to meal delivery services.

While it only takes a few seconds to hang up a coat or put keys and sunglasses in a basket or drawer, when in the midst of change, the time it takes to organize your home also changes. Some of the details will have to be put on hold. You will have plenty of time to work on efficiently getting your home in order after the fray is over. Focus on the important matters at hand that arose from outside your schedule and don't worry about what you think you should be doing. Having your home and schedules in order in the first place will make taking on new challenges more efficient.

All that is required is a new perspective and some discipline that just might turn into a different way of doing things. Don't let change create a disorganized lifestyle. Be flexible, be creative, and be open.

Be flexible, be creative, and be open.

Celebrate

Life requires order, order gives you freedom, and freedom leads to a more fulfilling life. When order is interrupted, you have to adjust, use discipline, allow yourself to wait, and have the willingness to change your behavior as well as your routine. Plan for change. Be cognizant of your valuable time and space. Make organizing fun instead of a chore. Give yourself something to look forward to when the job is done, then CELEBRATE!.

Celebrate your creativity, your ability to conquer potentially stressful situations. Celebrate your improved living space, your time management skills, and your decision-making prowess. Celebrate your new-found additions to your schedule like, allowing time for yourself and organizing your home.

You are strong, you are capable, and you are now more aware. So, pull up your reserves to handle those unexpected situations and don't let them scramble your brain. Prepare yourself with a new way of thinking which will definitely give you a reason to celebrate.

It's as simple as that!

Acknowledgments

Compassion is the most important attribute a professional organizer can have in their toolbox. Confusion Solution and other organizing services are dedicated to helping people in need of someone to lead them into relief. There are no set rules except for providing support and order. It is with a grateful heart that I thank all those in my life who led me to an industry composed of caring professionals.

I learned from my mother how to handle a move and the loss of things she had to leave behind. I learned how to manage a business through my 13 years in the corporate workplace, my enterprises; Romp & Circumstance and Merchandising Resources, and all the temp jobs in between. I learned by listening, observing, and understanding the significance of change from organizing professionals and authors. And, I have learned from my clients about how they live and their expectations for change.

I want to thank my sister Debbie for introducing me to the idea that inspired me to decide to become a professional organizer. I thank Alie and Michael Koth, Julia Parker, BNI, San Pedro Networking Group, Brad Lyon, Rick Plumley, Don Hammond, and a host of San Pedro's business professionals, my illustrator Amber Luecke, editor Spike E., and Kathryn Wilking who helped me get the word out.

Thanks to Organizers Julie Morgenstern, Ninna Atkins, Peter Walsh, Miriam Gold of Gold Standard Organizing, Sheryl Blue of Blues Moon, Professional Organization. And, I wish to honor the friends who supported me during the writing of this book, Teena, Laurie, Matt, Ted, and Susan.

This book was written to inspire others faced with change who desire a more organized life. As I continue to strive for new ways of bringing hope to a cluttered world, I look forward to the changes that surely will come.

CPSIA information can be obtained
at www.ICGtesting.com
Printed in the USA
BVHW022243250721
612854BV00005B/57